He Said,

She Said

Marriage, Divorce & Restoration

ERNEST 'DAVE' & ROSELINE 'ROZ'
BENNERMAN

Ignite Publishing
New Port Richey, FL 34652

ISBN-10: 0-9976639-0-1
ISBN-13: 978-0-9976639-0-7

Contents

Acknowledgments

We would like to dedicate this book to those who have been challenged in their marriage and for those who are taking the step to enter into this covenant agreement. If you've been struggling in your marriage, fighting for what you know is worth the fight, then we encourage you to continue reading. No, we're not perfect, but we've tried fighting in our own strength, which left us with a history of an eight-year failed marriage, ten-year divorce, and now we've taken a stance against the enemy which tries to come against our marriage.

We want to first thank our heavenly Father our Creator, Jesus Christ our Savior and the Holy Spirit our Comforter for being our Strength and Redeemer through this journey.

There are no words to say but thank you to our mothers, for being strong women in our lives who have shown us unconditional love. Rest in Peace, we miss and will always love you mom (Harriet Boyd – Roz's mom); and thank you mother (Mary B. Bennerman – Dave's mom), we love you very much.

Thank you, dad (Ernest C. Bennerman) for dropping nuggets of wisdom during the latter part of your life on earth before you departed to be with the Lord. We love You Dad, Rest in Peace; you will always be missed.

We want to thank our son (Terrell N. Bennerman) who is a very talented young man who is determined and purposed to impact this world. We love you, son.

I want to thank each one of my (Roz's) siblings, Tyrone, Keisha, Quentin (Rest in Peace), and Dennis (Rest in Peace) for your love, laughter and your encouragement. Thank you both for being so supportive, Tyrone and Keisha. May God continue to bless you and your families.

I want to thank each one of my (Dave's) sisters, Andrea and Tameka, for your laughter and encouragement; I love you ladies always, as well as my brother Anthony. I'm praying that he will be all God called him to be.

We want to thank our families for being supportive through all the transitions that we've journeyed through. We know our transitions did not only affect us, but those we love, so we give our heartfelt *Thank You* to our grandparents, uncles, aunts, nieces, nephews, cousins and friends for your love and support.

We thank Rev. Ronald B. Christian (Rest in Peace) who married us and Pastors Charles H. and Peggy B. Jones for pre-marriage counseling before we took the steps to remarry. We thank Apostle Mark T. Jones and Lady Lisa Jones of Center for Manifestation for your marriage development through the "It Takes 3" ministry. We also thank Pastors Ronnie and Krystal Stewart of the

Refuge Church for your covering as we embark into this new chapter in our lives.

Last but not least, we thank the enemy who has shown us that God's Word prevails over all of its devices. The bible says in Genesis 50:20 (NLT), "You intended to harm me, but God intended it all for good. He brought me to this position so I could save the lives of many people".

What the enemy meant for bad, God turned it around for His Glory!

A Personal Note from Dave and Roz

What is it like being married to me?

This is a great question! Whether married for only a brief period of time, many years, or even decades, this is a great question to assess, strengthen, and enhance marriages.

This is a question we continually ask ourselves. As you will discover while reading our book, this was not always the case. This was not asked until after 8 years of a failed marriage and 10 years of divorce; by the glory of God, we've been given the opportunity, currently married for 8 successful years, to ask this question. Yes, this is our second time around.

Our reason for writing this book is to encourage other married, and soon to be married couples, to ask this same question, **"What is it like being married to me?"**

Although we want our marriages to be the best they can be, sometimes, the simplest things can either strengthen or hinder our marriages. And we say this because we've been on both sides of the spectrum. But we thank God for allowing us to gain the wisdom and understanding to put things into their proper perspective concerning our marriage.

The title was inspired by the Holy Spirit; because of this, our book is formatted strategically to give you, our reader, a clear understanding of our perception of marriage, past and present. Each chapter is divided into subtitles, based on our individual perspective.

Our prayer is that, as we share our experiences with you through this book, you'll be encouraged to fight for your marriage and you too will ask the question, **"What is it like being married to me?"** *not once, but throughout the life of your union.*

Chapter 1

What Is Marriage?
Skewed to Defined

"God created marriage. No government subcommittee envisioned it. No social organization developed it. Marriage was conceived and born in the mind of God." Max Lucado

Dave

I can't believe how quickly the seasons come and go. As I look outside my door, I can't help but admire the beauty God has created for our enjoyment. I notice the birds singing, the squirrels playing, and children dancing in the city park, as I take a long pause and think back over the years to where God had placed my family and me.

Unfortunately, when I think about marriage I've noticed that many couples have a faulty foundation, and I was no different. And because of that faulty foundation, everything that could go wrong did go wrong. Typically, a husband and wife enjoy each other and keep smiling when they're sheltered from reality. I believe that's what Roz and I had, coming from two very different backgrounds as well as single parent homes. We were raised by single mothers, who did an incredible job raising us to be well respected individuals with strong family ties, which is very important to us. Once we moved from that covering, we were open season for the enemy to come against us because of our lack of knowledge.

I realize now that part of that lack of knowledge stemmed from not having a father in my life growing up. A father with vision is very important in a child's life, and the enemy's main goal is to remove the fathers from the home or distract them from the vision for their family. Fathers, what type of person do you want to be? We have a son; his name is Terrell. He has grown up to be a fine young man; he is 22 years old as we write this book. God is using him in so many ways. He has a gift of art and fashion that leaves me speechless. My role in his life is for him to witness what a kingdom man is supposed to be like in his everyday life.

I lacked vision during our first marriage. Everything was great, until money, bills, family, and work were not in their proper place; I neglected quality time with my wife. I remember the story of Moses in Exodus 9:1. God told Moses to tell Pharaoh, "Let my people go." The Israelites were living a life of slavery under the mighty hand of Pharaoh, picking mud and straw to make bricks. As the Israelites lived a life of slavery, I felt like I was, too...uncertain about my future, working hard to pay the bills during these difficult times. Husbands, what about your personal straw and mud? Do you labor much and receive only little? Are you working long hours so you can provide a good quality of life for your family? See, that was my reality at the time, but I was neglecting the time and responsibility to strengthen my family.

Here's my reason for collaborating with my wife in writing this book—to strengthen marriages and to educate those who are looking to get married. You have couples who give away their power in these dark days. The world says, if it feels good, do it. But as a man, we must know who we are as a person and, equally important, have a clear vision for where we're leading our family. Fellas, you must ask yourself: Who am I and where am I going? I sought ungodly advice from people who did not have any investment in our marriage. I believe somebody who's reading this book may be experiencing the same thing; it's time to tell the truth and shame the devil.

Roz and I want you to learn from our history. I'm here to inform you that, after being married for 8 years to this incredible woman the first time, my lust for other things, like cars, clothes, and women, during the latter part of our marriage eventually ended in a divorce. "When you have two heads doing the thinking for you, you have created a monster." You have to be set free from the opinions of others. I was so foolish to bring shame upon my wife and child during that dark time in my life. After 10 years of divorce, God miraculously led us back together; we've been remarried now, going on 9 years, and madly "In Love with Jesus."

Marriage really starts after the honeymoon is over; you still have to live with each other and decide what side of the bed you want to sleep on. You have to deal with issues, such as leaving the toilet seat up, *fellas*. My wife and I will show you what happens when you don't have God as your absolute truth and don't allow Him to govern your lives.

Our first marriage of 8 years was like asking my parents for the car keys at 9 years old: "too young to drive." I believe it's vital not to grow up too soon when it's time to make grown folk decisions, and to realize you're not just looking out for yourself, but for a wife and possibly children. But I had no proper understanding about marriage; I wanted every day to be like Disney World. Years ago, I can even remember the cereal commercial with a "Silly Rabbit" talking about "Trix are made for kids." There are so many couples doing silly things to tear down a good marriage. Do you know somebody who has had ungodly relationships before marriage? Fellas, can you think back to all the pornographic images you stored up, people from all over the world, black, white, Asian, Hispanic…we can go on and on. You must free your mind and body from soul ties before you get into a serious relationship.

To live a life of victory, you will have to remove all the boyfriends, ex-wives, ex-husbands, toxic family members, toxic friends, X-rated movies, gifts from each person you were involved with, etc., so you can take action. Break any ungodly soul ties from your history before you begin a new journey with the wife or husband of your dreams. Stop looking for perfection and proceed to excellence.

So many times the first thought that enters a person's mind are the outer appearances of the person they're searching for. But I want to encourage you to look beyond the outer appearance and consider if that person is evenly yoked with you. A couple of questions to consider for this purpose: "Is this person of the same faith?", "What are their ambitions, goals and aspirations?" And for all my sisters, as you're preparing yourself to allow a man to enter your life, consider this scripture from Proverbs 18:22 (NKJV), "He who finds a wife finds a good thing, and obtains favor from the LORD." So in other words, the man will find you…don't go searching for a man. Sisters, you might be looking for a Denzel Washington, Brad Pitt; or my brothers, you may be looking for a Taylor Swift, or Beyoncé. But suppose God has someone totally opposite from who you're looking for?

Here's a perfect example of how man looks at the outside, but God looks at the heart and the purpose of a person. The bible says in 1 Samuel 13:14, David was after God's own heart. David was tending the sheep; the prophet Samuel went to Jesse to see who would be the next king. He looked at all seven of Jesse's boys, and some were probably flexing their muscles, hoping they would be anointed by the prophet. But Samuel asked, "are these all the sons you have? There is still the youngest, Jesse replied. But he's out in the field watching the sheep and goats" (I Samuel 16:11). See, David stayed in the presence of God, as he was a worshiper. God will not bring Tall,

Dark, and Handsome, who has no relationship with Him. God is not moved by our needs, but by our faith.

We invite you to find a quiet place, sit back, and allow us to take you on a guided tour for having an incredible marriage, not because it's perfect, but because we decided to love each other unconditionally in word and deed. Most people talk about a good marriage, but you must take action so others can see what a good marriage looks like.

Here, we will address many obstacles, challenges, failures, and victories from our own experience, from which you can gain insight into what many marriages will face. We're here to equip you and to help you maintain your sanity and fall in love again. We'll share with you some keys you can pass along to your friends and family; hopefully, they will run to you for answers regarding their marriages, or maybe they are about to embark on marriage in the coming days, weeks, months, or years. It's critical that you understand how to build your most precious commodity, and it's by having the right perspective based on biblical principles.

Roz

Our perception and interpretation of marriage was skewed. Because of this ignorance, we experienced many challenges in our marriage.

Let me take you back to a time when we were so much in love and thought we knew what marriage was. I will give you my definition as I defined it during the years prior to 1988. Although I heard the words from the pastor, who married us, I did not fully understand the significance or challenges that awaited us. Yep, I was googly eyes over my husband and was super excited about *'the idea of marriage.'*

My definition of marriage was a man and woman who love each other, grow old together, have intercourse, and have children. Pretty vague, right? Well, that was my mindset. Fast forward to 1994, where all hell is breaking loose and we didn't seek counseling; instead, we remained in a place of ignorance and struggle.

Now, I define marriage as a sacred union between a man and woman, who join together to become one. They're joining together to love, cherish, respect, enjoy, prosper together, and to represent the union God has with the church. Because I'm a believer, I'm going to share what the bible says about marriage. The bible states in Genesis 2:22-24 (NLT), "Then the Lord God made a woman from the rib, and he brought her to the man. At last! the man exclaimed. This one is bone from my bone, and flesh from my flesh! She will be called woman, because she was taken from man. This explains why a man leaves his father and mother and is joined to his wife, and the two are united into one."

There was a disparity between what I believed during our first marriage versus the current. There was a state of ignorance, although fun times; we failed to seek counsel for or even confront the problems we were experiencing. Just picture a rug where you sweep everything you don't want to deal with under it. Yes, a mountain of mess. That's exactly what our skewed marriage was.

There's no one size fits all, but there is a blueprint on which to base our foundation...the word of God!

The bible gives a clear understanding of how a man should care for his wife and how a wife should care for her husband. But these were things we did not understand or seek to understand.

You'll notice, throughout this book, Dave and I turn the spotlight on ourselves. We had to take responsibility for our own actions, because it takes two people to create a marriage, which means we had to be intentional and do an introspection of ourselves.

We quickly found that marriage is not about changing the other person, although we tried and, needless to say, we failed miserably. But when I look back, I wonder why in the world I would try to change the man I married? It was because of who he is and the uniqueness of how God created him to be that I fell in love with him.

Eight years of marriage, 10 years of divorce, but as we write this book, we can say we've been married for 8 wonderful years. Don't get us wrong; we have our challenges and disagreements as any couple does, but our perspective has changed on how we respond to the challenges. Wherever there's more than one person, you will have more than one opinion.

We are now a student of each other. We can look back and know that being a 'student of each other' was an element of our previous marriage we did not practice. We had to learn, and we continue to learn, each other's love language. Although there are foundational truths about a wife in her desire to feel secure, loved, understood, and intimate, and for the husband to feel respected, honored, and to have sex, there are many other needs; but these, I believe, are the basic core needs of each individual in a marriage.

And one of the core needs I would like to expound on is **sex** and how it's not only **Pleasurable** but a **Necessity** in a married couple's life (unless there's medical conditions that prohibit it). God created us as sexual human beings who are designed to procreate the earth (Genesis 1:28). And it's through sex that we can fulfill this mandate. Because God calls his creation to procreate the earth, that means *there's nothing wrong with sex between a husband and wife.* Not only is sex a mandate, but a healthy sex life has incredible health benefits. Did you know that sex is based on vascularity (blood flow)? And being a fitness enthusiast, I must share a common way to increase and sustain vascularity; it's through maintaining a lifestyle of exercise and healthy eating. When both spouses take health and fitness seriously, it helps to increase their blood flow and energy levels, helps avoid unwanted visits to the doctor, helps reduce stress in their life, and increases sexual intimacy versus someone who is overweight.

God has called marriage to be a fulfilling union between a man and woman, but it's up to us as married couples to make the effort to keep our marriages healthy and strong in every area of our life (spiritually, emotionally, physically and financially).

Questions to Ponder

1. How do you define marriage?

2. Did you enter marriage believing your spouse would complete you? What did you discover after the marriage ceremony was over?

3. Do you have supportive, mature, God fearing married couples you can confide in?

4. Are you a 'student of your spouse'? Do you make understanding your spouse's love language a priority in your life?

5. Do you and your spouse make health and physical fitness a part of your lifestyle?

Chapter 2

Let's Start from the Beginning

"And we know that God causes everything to work together for the good of those who love God and are called according to his purpose for them." Romans 8:28 (NLT)

Dave

I can remember September of 1982, working part-time at a car wash after school, when I noticed this beautiful young lady riding with another young lady, whom I later found out was her cousin, staring back at me like she wanted me all to herself. Okay, maybe not like that, but you get the point.

"Hey baby girl, if you want your change, you need to give me your phone number," is what I said.

Guess what? She gave me her phone number. She was trying to give me the wrong number. But, yes, she gave me the correct one.

I was on cloud nine; I invited her to my 16th birthday party. I wanted every song to be a slow song. That's what young boys think about. We played songs, like 'It's Going to Take a Miracle' by Denise Williams, 'Fire and Desire' by Rick James and Tina Marie, wow! Puppy love was the lord of my life. She dumped me three months later, after we went to the New Edition and Grand Master Flash Concert. It is no wonder that, to this day, when I bring up the concert, she says she doesn't remember any concert like that at all. Life can be comical when you look back on how goofy we were.

"Roz, I worked all week at the car wash to make that money to pay for those tickets," is what I told her, but it made no difference.

Oh well, that's the way my life had gone in the early days.

After my 16th birthday, I spent several years trying to figure out what I wanted to do with my life. Eventually, I joined the military and later went to college. I met several people during this time, and I found myself involved in foolish relationships, playing foolish games. It seemed like, every time I took two steps forward, I would take three steps backwards. The bible says in Hosea 4:6a (NKJV), "My people are destroyed for lack of knowledge." When you're blind spiritually, your only course of action is trying to lead others on the same path.

Although I experienced setbacks, five years after we dated the first time, Roz and I met on the bus, during our college years; exchanged numbers and decided to catch up. We started dating, hanging out, and enjoying each other's company. We fell in love after about 1 year of courtship. We loved and cared for each other, so I believed in my heart we knew each other well enough to take a leap of faith and move on to the next level.

So after our first year of dating, I struck up enough nerve to ask her to marry me, right inside Golden Corral. I figured lunch time was as good a time as any. I pulled out her engagement ring and said to her, "Look, Roz, I love you and I want to spend the rest of my life with you." Roz paused for a moment, and it seemed like an hour before she finally gave me her answer: 'I will!' I left that all-you-can-eat restaurant, feeling like I was on cloud nine.

Not everyone was as excited about this marriage union on which we were about to embark. As I write this book, I know we should have waited and not been in such a hurry to get married, but all the trials and disappointments made me a better person.

We both wanted to fulfill our goals and dreams, but "Lust" was the god I served at that time. I can remember a famous song in the 80's by Tina Turner, called "What's Love Got to Do with It?" I was a very self-centered, prideful, fearful, insecure person. Have I left out anything else? Yeah, I was like a dog in heat. I thought, like most men getting married, I can have all the sex I desire from this woman, since we're spending the rest of our lives together. I want to stop right there for a moment...how about you? Have you married your wife or husband so you can enjoy *only* the sexual pleasures between two people who love, sorry "Lust" each other, until the other person says no? The word 'NO' has caused more divorces and unfaithfulness in marriages than you can imagine.

My perception of marriage, without Godly counseling, had major flaws. We tried to build our life with a faulty philosophy of what a marriage was supposed to be. Don't use Play Doh as patching material, when you find a crack in your concrete (marriage); metaphorically, that's what we tried to do. You must invest in the real thing if you're going to have a stable marriage. We were both very immature people, who rejected the idea of walking with God. I don't want to use that as an excuse, because statics show that many people in the church get divorced also. We had no clue what a healthy, strong marriage should be, nor did we realize what sacrifices had to be made. I was a mess; I played the role of how a husband was supposed to act. I should have won an Oscar for my performance of "Fake it till you make it." Instead, we should have been 'Faithing' it; believing and taking intentional steps to make it a success.

My marriage counselor during our first marriage was Al Bundy from the sitcom "Married with Children." Pretty funny if you remember that sitcom, right? Just a synopsis if you're not familiar with it, they had quite the dysfunctional marriage. They would find fault with each other constantly. I can remember during the first few months of our marriage, although there were some great times, just like the sitcom, we started fault-finding and doing just enough to stay out of each other's way. We were struggling to make ends meet, going from one dead end job to the next. During this time, I started searching for somebody, who made it, with the type of lifestyle I wanted to obtain. I looked for my dad; however, he had his own challenges. I'm sure you know someone whose footsteps you'd like to follow in. But, be careful when you say you want to walk in someone's footsteps; the question to ask yourself is, "Am I willing to pay the price and make the necessary sacrifices?" Even with marriage, we have to ask this same question, "Am I willing to pay the price and make the necessary sacrifices to have a successful marriage?" Remember, marriage requires constant sacrifice and compromise. You have to go into marriage understanding and being truthful with yourself when answering this question.

Be willing to sit down and talk about the sacrifices. Because as you sit and talk you'll discover even more about each other's needs, goals, and dreams, collectively and individually. Each of you will find your place within the life you're looking to have together. Sad to say, but I believe the media has done a horrible job of portraying the husband and wife in the home. With so many distractions bombarding our minds as husbands and fathers, if we're not careful, we will head toward a train wreck. And it's so important, as a man and woman according to the Bible, to get your parents' blessings or someone you trust to tell you the truth, whether you like it or not. Others may see what we don't see.

Seeking someone else's advice or blessing can help avoid a marriage that simply starts out on fire, and then suddenly fizzles out. Many times, the fizzle starts to happen when we simply tolerate our spouses, instead of celebrate them. Although there will be times when your spouse's attitude will push your buttons, you have to find the motivation to look beyond their attitude. Here's something that, if applied well, will give you tremendous results. Take a mental picture of your spouse and see how wonderful they are despite their flaws; see the uniqueness of how God wired them. Most couples, who don't see eye-to-eye, love to get even, rather than get ahead. Stop the foolishness, take a look at the blueprint (the Bible) and live a life of fullness.

Finding the motivation to look beyond the attitude and the flaws was something I had to learn. But I thank God this is my mindset now. Yes, many of life's trials and tribulations will rock the very foundation if you don't have a clear revelation of where your marriage is going. But now as we step into our present, Roz and I made up our minds to have our marriage look less like the world and more like Christ. The bible says in Mark 10:9 (NLT), "Let no one split apart what God has joined together." The key word in this scripture is 'let' which is a word of volition, meaning power of using one's will. In other words, we are able to stand against someone or temptations trying to split apart what God has joined together.

When you see your spouse as your greatest blessing from God you will stand firmly on this scripture (Mark 10:9). I'm thankful because now I do see my wife as one of my greatest blessings from God; He has given me the right one to refine, shape, and mold me into the Man of God you see today. A real man opens more than the door for his wife; he opens the door to his heart. The bible says in Revelation 3:20 (NLT), "Look! I stand at the door and knock. If you hear my voice and open the door, I will come in, and we will share a meal together as friends." As, in this scripture, when a friend sits and has a meal with a friend, they're open to heartfelt conversation with one another. As married couples we must have that same openness in our marriages.

Openness will help keep the fire burning in your marriage, but you will only be open if you believe in the vision for your marriage; your **WHY** for being married. This is what Roz and I are stressing throughout this book. And for those soon to be married couples, I want you to take your time to get to know each other before you take the next step. We want you to plan and stand firm for better or worse. You will know the right mate to marry; just don't settle because the person has a pretty face or maybe the brother is big and strong. We want you to marry for the right reasons. Remember, what you do will affect not only your life and your husband or wife's life, but also your children's lives.

If you are single, be selective when sharing your soul with someone you are dating. I want you to try the 60-day rule.

60 Day Rule

1) Week 1 – Communication: limit time on the phone per call...10 to 15 minutes each day. Go out for coffee/lunch. **No Sex Talk**

2) Week 2 – Communication: Limit time on the phone to 10 to 15 minutes each day. Date Night: Men, you want to open doors and pull up chair (ask permission to pay for the meal). **No Sex Talk**

3) Week 3 – Communication: Limit time on the phone to 10 to 15 minutes each day. Talk about what your friend likes to do (goals, dreams, etc.). **No Sex Talk**

4) Week 4 – Date Night: Gather data from the weeks before and meet his/her needs by going to the museum, theater, dinner, etc. Communication: 20 to 30 minutes each day. **No Sex Talk**

5) Week 5 - See if you can meet his/her friends. (You want to see the company they keep. How do they act around you?) Communication: 20 to 30 minutes each day. **No Sex Talk**

6) Week 6 – Communication: 20 to 30 minutes each day. **No Sex Talk**

7) Week 7 – Date Night: Be about ½ hour late for the date (you want to see how this individual handles crisis or disappointments). **No Sex Talk**

8) Week 8 – Communication: 30 to 45 minutes each day. Have a conversation about the previous week. You want their honest assessment of this relationship. **No Sex Talk**

You did your homework, so now take time and give this person a mental evaluation. You're special, so take your time and don't be pressured to move forward. **No Sex Talk.**

Through this 60-Day lesson you will have discovered some of the aspirations, goals, dislikes, and temperament of this person you're considering marrying. The 'No Sex Talk' is an excellent way to know if it's just lust for this person or if you're able to establish a deeper, more meaningful relationship. Overall, it gives you both time to go beyond the physical attraction only.

Roz

When we say "I do," we enter a covenant agreement, which are promises, responsibilities, and privileges based on biblical principles. And as we share our story, you'll discover how we initially did not understand the significance of this covenant agreement. We were young and did not seek wise counsel about marriage; I'm not making excuses, but this was simply our experience. We were not saved during our first marriage, and the reason I state this is because, now, we are believers, and the fabric of this book and our marriage is based on our beliefs. The Word of God is our foundation for our marriage. The Bible states in Ecclesiastes 4:12 (NLT), "A person standing alone can be attacked and defeated, but two can stand back-to-back and conquer. Three are even better, for a triple-braided cord is not easily broken." It's because of the Word of God that we give all praise, because without the Word, we literally can say we would not have gotten remarried. This scripture helps us remember that we're not alone; our strength is 3-fold, in and through the challenges we face.

Here we go. Back when bell bottoms and the Jheri Curl were in style. Dave and I had it too. We met in September of 1982 at a car wash where Dave worked. I was with my cousin taking care of errands, and one of those was to wash the car. Dave, in his smooth but corny way, told my cousin as she approached him for change for the manual car wash machine he wouldn't give her the change, unless I came to get it. I'm laughing as I write, because he asked for my number, and instead of me giving him a bogus number, I gave him the correct number; I'm so happy I did.

So I gave him my number and as time went on, we dated as young people normally do. We held hands while going to the movies, parks, and restaurants. I was thrilled when Dave invited me to his 16th birthday party. We had such a great time, but I must share an embarrassing, but funny, situation that happened during the party. It was a house party at Dave's house, and of course, the lights were turned low. Can you just picture a house full of teenagers with the lights down low? Well, what happened brought the party to a streaking halt. We had on slow jams, a little Luther Vandross, Anita Baker, and all the good music, and someone leaning against the wall fell through. Yes, the wall had a hole in it. Dave's mom came out, and I tell you, we could not get out of that house fast enough.

That situation is something we still laugh about to this day.

We dated for a couple of months, then lost touch. But in 1986, we connected again after seeing one another on the public transit #13 bus. We grew up in urban New Jersey, where we had convenient access to public transportation. As I think back, I truly believe this was divine timing.

As we reacquainted ourselves, we discovered an intimate connection. While in college, we started out occasionally speaking over the phone, and then it advanced to occasional dating. We were both focused on our studies, but also discovered a more intimate and passionate love for one another.

In 1988, we believed our love was so strong that we decided to get married, although this was not the most favorable decision amongst our parents, because they believed we were too young; they said if we were so in love, there should not be an issue waiting until after we graduated college to marry. As we look back now, they were correct.

We married on August 26, 1988 at Beulah Baptist Church in Newark, NJ. It was far from a big wedding, but it didn't matter; we were in love. We started good as newlyweds, enjoying each other's company and hanging out with friends. We had no kids, so we were free to come and go as we chose. We had a great marriage on the surface. I say on the surface, because we never asked the question, "What is it like being married to me?" Not asking this question was our downfall.

We dealt with all the surface stuff, you know...go to work, pay bills, and of course, the intimate sexual times. We didn't focus on strengthening our relationship, and we eventually began to lose touch with each other.

Unfortunately, when we set ourselves to the task of trying to 'fix' a failing marriage, we didn't realize the accumulation of problems we needed to deal with. We didn't bother to look at the strengths, qualities, and characteristics that brought us together in the first place. Whether we had been married for one year or twenty years, we discovered this neglect of strength, qualities, and characteristics were relevant to improve our marriage.

This should have been obvious to us, but we didn't use wisdom to see beyond the faults of one another.

What brought you and your spouse together? What accounted for you and him/her making the decision to spend the rest of your lives together? Whether you and your spouse were starry-eyed young people who married after knowing each other for a very brief period of time, or whether you had been in each other's lives for many years, let your memory take you back to your beginning to remember the love you had for one another when you decided to marry in the first place.

We found that it's important to identify the qualities and characteristics we find the most appealing in each other. Re-entering marriage, we found we needed to know the goals, hopes, plans, and dreams we both had, individually and collectively. Some answers were very similar, and there were many that were different, but the questions had to be addressed to establish an understanding of each other's hopes, and aspirations. And through this process, we learn the qualities and characteristics that we admire and hold onto, which can be brought back to memory in the tough times.

If you're married, we want to encourage you if (or when) you encounter tough times, no matter how hopeless your situation may seem, to take this little trip down Memory Lane. It is one of the most important steps you can take in remembering your **'WHY'** for getting married. It is likely that you will find that the factors that influenced your decision to marry still exist; they just need to be noticed again and rekindled!

Also, while you are thinking about these factors, you may also recall many things you and your spouse shared back then. You may have loved taking part in some kind of activity you both enjoyed, but somewhere along the line, other priorities started to take precedence, and you no longer made time for these things.

One of the major things that happened as we reengaged with one another was the excitement we shared talking about our shared interests. We enjoyed participating in sports and having picnics in the park; those activities we mutually enjoyed were bonding experiences. And if you're dealing with challenges in your marriage, remember there is no reason you cannot do the same; **rekindle the passion you had for one another**.

Going back to our beginning allowed us time to assess the strengths and interests we had in common. In doing so, we recalled the passion we had for our relationship and for each other. And when we did this, we were in a position to reclaim those things. The favorite pastimes, the goals and dreams, they were all still there, waiting to be uncovered and appreciated again!

Questions to Ponder

1. Do you spend quality time with your spouse? For example, schedule time for date night to enjoy intimate time together.

2. How do you respond when your spouse says 'No' to sex? Are you still loving and understanding?

3. Do you have a vision for your marriage?

4. Do you try to fix your spouse?

5. Do you privately and publicly celebrate your spouse? Or are you consistently critical of them?

Chapter 3

Opening the Lines of Communication

"The goal in marriage is not to think alike, but to think together."
Robert C. Dodds

Dave

August 26, 1988: I can remember my beautiful bride walking down the aisle looking so graceful, so radiant I needed a pair of sunglasses to keep from going blind. All right, not quite like that. We were two fools, excited about spending a lifetime of marriage together. We thought we knew all the answers; our love would make up for plain stupidity. Don't get me wrong; I looked forward to spending my life with Roz, until she burned the toast or if she complained enough to work on my nerves; that's when I started to shrink back into my cocoon.

Our communication was great, as long as I did not have to talk long about things she considered important. Now, as long as it was about me, I wanted to talk until the crack of dawn. If you looked up the word selfishness in the dictionary, I am sure you would see a picture of me. I cared enough, until she stopped listening to me. Just like baseball, I was the type that would bring my bat, ball, bases and gloves and play until you irritated me. I did not include screaming and yelling in my definition of communication. I would close up when things got really heated. I had a hard time when confronted with anything that would highlight my weakness. I flunked love language class 101.

What about you, do you only care about expressing your opinion during a conversation with your spouse without listening to their opinion? Do you shy away from confrontation within your marriage? Well, that was me. I was what you called a runner. I would leave before things got too hot. Why, Dave? Because I was afraid to show how vulnerable I had become. See, it all starts with how you think about yourself. I thought little of myself. Most relationships I had in the past were fine, until the other person expressed their opinion.

We would have fall-outs over minor things, in my perspective, but they were very important to Roz. She is the type of person who loves to keep things in order, and I hated that back then. I made a major mistake in making sly remarks about things that were important to her, but petty to me. I had disorder in my life, blaming everyone else for things that kept falling apart in my life.

My mindset was, let's fake it till we make it. Roz would ask me; which direction are we headed? I would say,

"I don't know?" When should we save for a house? "I Don't Know?" My wife had her hands full with me. She should have taken that premarital class we both failed to inquire about the first time around; I'm sure it would have saved her a few years. When you have a history of talking fast to get your point across, you will care less what others have to say. Trust me; things will only get worse before they get better. Look back over your childhood and remember when you cried, because you did not get your way or because you wanted your favorite toy. Well, Roz and I faced a lot of challenges, like selfishness, which came from our childhoods.

As we got older, we needed to connect with wise married couples, instead of buying into the lie we should keep to ourselves, hoping things would work out for the better. No! I (and you) have to deal with my (your) lack of communication. You know what? I'm the type of person who enjoys conversing with people. I know I'm an extrovert. Roz is an introvert; she enjoys her quiet time, although she enjoys connecting with folks. I need to talk and engage folks from all walks of life. I love to hear their stories.

At times, my wife would tell me some chick was trying to hit on me, but I would take it as if Roz was trying to start a fight. I remember a look my mother had that you didn't want to mess with; Roz has the same look. She had a look that would cut through your soul. Can I ask you a question, husbands and wives? Does your body language send mixed signals affecting your marriage? Do you want to give your spouse a hug after coming home from a hard day at the office, but their body language says, "You Better

Back Up!" Then maybe the husband or wife storms out of the house into the parking lot, looking for a drink or a cigarette. Hey husband, hey wife, "DON'T GO THERE!" Do you see the danger signs?

When we wrote about, "What is Marriage?" in the first chapter, it's clear you must have a clear revelation of marriage from God's point of view. We have an enemy who is unseen, looking forward to tripping us up; the danger signs are evident everywhere you turn. Fellas! Don't walk out of the house, saying to yourself, my wife doesn't understand me; I will get a drink at the bar, or at the club; maybe I will find someone who understands me. Danger!!! You are walking on the edge of the building; you need somebody like me, who will tell you the truth, in love, to get your butt back inside the house where it's safe. The only people you find walking on the edge without a safety belt are daredevils or someone who's ready to end their life. I was this person, because I associated lack of communication with rejection.

I equated rejection with self-worth. Not realizing at that time that rejection does not diminish my value as a person. When I pulled back the layers, as if peeling an onion, I discovered one dysfunctional thought overlaying another. It wasn't until I meditated on the word of God that I realized my thoughts were self-defeating. The bible says in Ephesians 4:23 (NLT), "Instead, let the Spirit renew your thoughts and attitudes." You have to lose your mind and take on the mind of Christ. All the bells and whistles are going off, but you're so diluted in your thinking because of the drugs, alcohol, or sex that your senses become numb.

Did you know, you can quit on your marriage before you physically leave the building? See, I'm from New Jersey. We would go downtown, and when the stores were ready to close, they would flip the closed sign in the window, bring down the metal security doors, and secure the premises. You can talk to those metal storm doors if you want, but I'm here to tell you, you're not getting in. I use this analogy to let you know how important it is to have open communication. Surrender your will and take on God's will. How often do you need to be separated or divorced before you drop your pride and open the door to communication?

When you have two people with different personalities and perspectives, you will have some disagreements and heated moments. Make sure, married people, not to go to bed angry! The bible says in Ephesians 4:26 (NLT), "And don't sin by letting anger control you. Don't let the sun go down while you are still angry." You cannot have a one-sided argument. Picture your car having a flat on one side. Your vehicle will lean more on one side; you're limited at this point.

Communication is key to holding a marriage together. Things changed for me when I stepped into my wife's shoes and saw what she saw. Take some time to sit down with your mate and find a resolution to the madness that's going on in your mind. Here are some keys to help handle confrontations; they worked for me.

1. Never keep quiet (silent treatment)

2. Never come to conclusions

3. Get to the facts (no guessing games)

4. Focus on the major problem (don't bring up past relationships)

5. Use wisdom when discussing matters with relatives

6. Talk in the present tense, not past tense

7. Try to talk to each other with respect (no screaming, yelling, cursing, name calling)

Always keep your communication lines open and you will have tremendous success in your marriage.

Roz

In order for any relationship to be successful, there must be consistent, effective communication. Although this is true for any relationship, it is most essential in marriage. In nearly every marriage that has begun to deteriorate, based on statistics, lack of communication is towards the top of the list.

One of the best ways to resolve this problem is to go back to the very beginning, your beginning! This was an area Dave and I realized was the pitfall of our first marriage. We were not truthful in our concerns with different areas of our life, including marriage. We simply lacked effective communication!

Our relationship was more about sweeping things (concerns) under the rug. Can you relate to this one? Let me give you a visual. Think of the formation of mountains. They are formed from the crust colliding (personalities clashing); cracks (those areas in a marriage not resolved before going to bed); crumbles (how a marriage deteriorates due to breakdown in communication); folds (one situation or concern overlapping the true issue), and spews (when you reach your capacity to tolerate each other any longer). Now picture this happening for the last 2 years of our first marriage. Oh yes, a mountain of concerns, problems, and issues.

We didn't address our issues, and as a result, our marriage went downhill pretty quickly. But we didn't stop the sexual intimacy. In our fifth year of marriage, we had a heartrending experience, we had a miscarriage. But by the grace of God, the following year we gave birth to our son, Terrell. Regardless of all that we experienced, he is truly a blessing!

Don't get me wrong, there were enjoyable times during our marriage, but obviously, there could have been even better times.

During the final two years, there was a lot of distance between us, and I've learned that a man leaves a marriage 'before he leaves.' Let me explain what I mean by that. From my own experience and the experience of other married women, who are now divorced, I've learned that, once a man has resolved in his heart that his marriage is not worth the effort any longer, his emotions have left the marriage, although his physical body is still there; he's dedicated, but not committed to the relationship. But if one of us had noticed and confronted the disconnect that took place, we could have refused to allow the enemy and ourselves to destroy or hinder the progression of our marriage. The dedication and commitment, coupled with unconditional love, would have sought the help, counseling, whatever it took, to find a resolution.

As we write, we are experiencing 8 years of a successful marriage, and with that, we have found that one of the most important ingredients in marriage is

'Effective Communication', but the first ingredient is to have the Word of God as the foundation of your marriage. The Bible says in Mark 10:9 (NLT), "Let no one split apart what God has joined together." This doesn't just mean outside temptations, but for each spouse to see themselves as the 'no one' in this scripture as well. Each spouse must take full responsibility for their marriage. And 'Effective Communication' is one key to avoiding the tearing apart of a marriage. We can say, unfortunately, we experienced a lack of effective communication, but to the Glory of God, we can use our testimony to encourage and strengthen other marriages that may have challenges in this area.

Now we continue to study each other, and our relationship continues to evolve for the better.

Just a word of caution...if you and your spouse fall in the lack of communication category, it is essential that you come to terms with this problem so you can work on resolving it. Unfortunately, just as we did, we have encountered couples who experience lack of communication. They feel that "love can conquer all," and therefore, do not (and did not) recognize the need to discuss important issues; others have begun a relationship and even entered marriage, feeling unable to voice their thoughts, feelings, preferences, or beliefs, merely agreeing with their partners on everything.

For couples in this category, the time usually comes when they are no longer content to simply "go with the flow," and eventually, find that major differences and disagreements occur when they attempt to assert themselves. They may find that their spouse wishes to remain in charge, or they may find they and their spouse disagree on significant issues.

In either case, opening the lines of communication is the first, essential step in asserting oneself and to begin to reach agreements. You will find there will be a number of instances in which you and your spouse must "agree to disagree." We did not do this. We want to encourage other couples to avoid the same trap of the enemy we fell into. Not agreeing to disagree was an issue at the beginning of our first marriage, and with that came deterioration.

Sometimes, also, a person's priorities shift. While the marital relationship was once a person's number-one focus, other factors which he/she chose led the marriage to take second-place, causing it to not seem as important as it was at the beginning. In these instances, reassessing priorities is the main key to reestablishing good communication. It is necessary to give your marriage the time and attention it needs and deserves and to give your spouse the time and attention he or she needs and deserves.

We realize there are other instances in which people simply lack good communication skills. If this appears to describe you or your spouse, take heart; good communication skills can be learned. Even if you are non-assertive, or do not know how to communicate effectively, it is a skill you can learn with practice and experience. Some great suggestions, just to name a few, connect with a friend for debatable conversations; have them give you constructive feedback on how effectively you communicated. Perhaps, join your local Toastmasters, which is an awesome opportunity to assert yourself and receive constructive feedback also.

So if any of these categories describe you and your spouse, recognizing the foundation of the problem is the first step in resolving it. We're not sharing this because we're perfect, but because we've experienced this firsthand, and if there's anyone reading this, who we can encourage, that's exactly what we want to do.

We care deeply about marriages staying strong through life's challenges.

To sum up "Effective Communication" between a husband and wife, based on our own experience- you may add to it, but this sums it up for us- when you and your spouse can talk with each other about all important subjects, and even subjects which have no serious implications at all; when you can freely share what you think, feel, believe, want, like, and dislike; when you can state your stand on important issues and listen to your spouse with mutual respect, even when there are matters of disagreement, you can have good, "Effective Communication."

Dave and I have found that "Effective Communication" comes from practice, experience, respect, and the time you are willing to put into it!

<u>Questions to Ponder</u>

1. Can you be brutally honest and respectful with your spouse?

2. Do you discount what's important to your spouse?

3. Have you discussed how you will handle conflict in your marriage? Do you have clear guidelines that you and your spouse have agreed on?

4. Do you consistently reassess your priorities to make sure your marriage stays at the top of the list?

5. Do you know your spouse's personality traits? Do you allow them to reenergize based on their needs? Example…those who are more extroverted in their personality normally reenergize when engaging with other people; whereas, introverts normally need more solitude to reenergize.

Chapter 4

It's About Time

"Don't copy the behavior and customs of this world, but let God transform you into a new person by changing the way you think. Then you will learn to know God's will for you, which is good and pleasing and perfect." Romans 12:2 (NLT)

Dave

In the year, 1999, I walked through the church doors, holding my head down in shame, feeling rejected for a failed marriage of 8 years due to my own selfishness. The bible says in Proverbs 5:1-4a (NLT), "My son, pay attention to my wisdom; listen carefully to my wise counsel. Then you will show discernment, and your lips will express what you've learned. For the lips of an immoral woman are as sweet as honey and her mouth is smoother than oil. But in the end she is as bitter as poison." My fleshly desires led to my demise. Not only did I hurt myself, but I hurt my wife with my foolishness. I'd broken my vows, so in other words, I was a "Covenant Breaker." My name was no good at all, but there's someone who died on Calvary. His name is "Jesus." He removed my shame and dishonor and made me righteous. You guys are about to have me preach. He is the King of kings and Lord of lords.

Let's finish my story. As I sat in the back of the church, I was ready to run out the door, but the Holy Spirit led me to a little Baptist church to make a public confession to the congregation of believers. You should have seen me; I had on an Atlantic City T-Shirt with dice, with earrings in my ear, trying to be cool. I cried out with tears of joy as the whole church rejoiced as I joined the fellowship of believers. "It's About Time!" God placed people in my life to help me be the person He called me to be. He started cleaning my soulish man and connecting me with leaders who would love me unconditionally. Everything I believed about marriage, without the revelation of God, was skewed. The bible says in Ephesians 5:25 (NLT), "For husbands, this means love your wives, just as Christ loved the church. He gave up his life for her." The bible says in James 1:22 (NLT), "But don't just listen to God's word. You must do what it says. Otherwise, you are only fooling yourselves." Real men, who honor covenant, don't run from their vows. I had to step out in faith and keep moving forward to a place of restoration, the first step to wholeness, and stop blaming everyone with whom I connected for my failures. The Lord says, "It's About Time" you own up to your mistakes and understand what it means to be a husband.

Most men believe the lie that you have to be tough and macho, thinking you're God's gift to women. God is raising real men who love Him, who have decided to approach Him, regardless of their baggage. I know who I am in Christ Jesus. So, I want to let you know, "It's About Time" to man up, fellas, and be the man God called you to be; "It's About Time" you stop being the victim, "Man Up" and do an introspection of your issues. No more running, fellas; man up and show your wife, family, friends, and the world how to represent a Kingdom Marriage. The time is right now! "It's About Time" you write a new chapter; the past is the past, so hopefully, you've learned something and you truly repented (changed your mind). The bible says in 2 Corinthians 5:17 (KJV), "Therefore if any man be in Christ, he is a new creature: old things are passed away; behold, all things are become new." Praise God!

There might be somebody who has gone through some painful things with their spouse, due to emotional or physical abuse. The first step to recovery is to own up to your mistakes and deal with the consequences you brought on yourself. Right now, if you have some serious problems, you need to get your Pastor or seek professional counseling to get the proper healing. The first thing for me was to be alone, by myself, and find out about this man in the mirror.

I had to know my purpose first, and then have an understanding of God's plan concerning marriage. And His ultimate plan is to be fruitful and planted, as His kingdom is established. The bible says in Jeremiah 17:8 (NLT), "They are like trees planted along a riverbank, with roots that reach deep into the water. Such trees are not bothered by the heat or worried by long months of drought. Their leaves stay green and they never stop producing fruit."

Let me translate this in "Pookie version": Look here, Shanana, I will stay home and make sure the bills are paid, I'm not hanging with the crew, I will take care of my responsibility as the "Man" and father of this family, I'm not scared, and I don't care if people think of me as whipped. Baby! No more running out on you. I'm here no matter how hot things get up in here. I will not get desperate and go out to gamble or sell drugs. My hustle days are over, and I will keep a good job.

I think we get the point; relax, we're having a little fun. Loosen up!

Here are keys to help you get on track, so you can get a true revelation of your steps to be the husband or wife you were called to be.

1. Your Actions will always determine your belief regarding your marriage.

2. Prepare your field to receive the rain of an abundance of love, intimacy, and compassion.

3. Honor God with your Actions and Attitude toward your spouse.

4. It's easy to Lead when you are Strong; can you lead when you are down and things fall apart?

5. Give your best to your spouse and leave the rest to God.

Roz

In the seventh year of being divorced, enjoying the single life…dance clubs (I was not a stripper, but some of the outfits I wore…some people might have thought I was), boyfriends, and traveling...the time came when I knew there had to be more to my life than this. I decided to release the boyfriends and wean myself away from the dance club scene (this took time, because I enjoyed dancing, and just didn't want to let it go).

As I was going through this process, a dear childhood friend reentered my life. She and I have known each other for over 15 years. I was blown away at how much had changed between us. I was now a divorced, single mother with no clear direction of what the next chapter in my life would be, and she was saved and engaged to be married. So much time had passed that I was excited to catch up. So we started catching up, but what I heard was not what I expected…she started to share with me the love of Christ. Although I wasn't quite ready for all of this, I listened. Week after week, she shared different scriptures from the bible with me, and I became more intrigued. I started asking questions, because I just didn't understand.

Eventually, because of my intrigue with what she was sharing, I started to attend different churches…I was on a journey. I thought to myself, maybe this was something I needed. I attended church after church, but it never felt right, until after my hairstylist invited me to her Initial Sermon at Christian Love Baptist Church. I debated with myself about attending, but finally went. It was there that I discovered something different. Words were spoken that touched my innermost being. The Word of God was speaking to me, like I never heard before. After attending for the first time, I wanted more. So I continued to visit this church and was blown away by the worship, praise, and the words that came forth from the pastor, at that time, Rev. Ronald B. Christian (Rest in Peace). He showed such a great level of love and compassion for the members of the church. As I started to read the bible, I saw the unconditional love of Jesus Christ and realized this man of God was allowing the love of Christ to be exhibited through his life.

As I continued to attend church, it felt like the most exciting time I had experienced in my life. Eventually, attending bible study classes with my friend was part of my life on Friday nights, rather than hanging out at the dance club. There was a yearning in me for a greater understanding of what the bible said about my life. The club scene became less important, because my desire to understand the bible became a priority in my life. There was a great excitement in me to share the teachings and love of Christ with others.

Now, this was a time when Dave and I were much more cordial with one another. Because we had joint custody of our son, Dave would meet me every other Friday for his visitation with Terrell. As I mentioned previously, I was excited to share what I learned through the Word, and Dave was too. We started to share sermons from church services we attended the Sunday before. God was working in both of our hearts. I remember, one time, Dave telling me he'd been praying for me, and I was stunned. This surprised me, because I never thought he would include me in his prayer time.

As time went on, I couldn't resist any longer the desire in my heart to have more, to know more, and to allow Christ in my heart. I surrendered my life to Jesus Christ in 2000. And God began to speak to me about the areas of my life that were out of alignment with His will. He was chiseling away at those things that did not bring Him glory. The first alignment was to sit under the teaching of Rev. Christian, and I did so for seven years. This was a time of repentance, forgiveness, and restoration.

I realized that Christ was freeing me from the bondage of unforgiveness that I didn't realize I had in my heart toward Dave. This was the start of the process of renewing my mind with the Word of God and releasing those things that hindered my progress. Unhealthy relationships had to be severed; although some were difficult, I made a choice to be obedient to what God was speaking to me. God replaced those relationships with men and women who edified and encouraged me through the Word. And right in time, because I needed the support and accountability; it was difficult to go from hanging out, drinking, and living any kind of way.

Many things started to unfold in my life. Unforgiveness seemed to be the most difficult thing to handle, now that it pressed on my heart. There were even women I encountered, who had gone through divorce and told me they felt abandoned and had unforgiveness toward their ex, and I was no different. No, I was not alone, but I didn't want to be in this position any longer. I realized that "I allowed" it to sit and fester inside me. The dance clubs and frivolous relationships were just a wall I built to cover up the bitterness and unforgiveness in my heart, and this put me in a state of bondage. No, I was not in a physical jail cell, but I was in an inner jail in my soul. The dance clubs and boyfriends were "hurt blockers" from the pain I felt after my divorce. The festering of bitterness and unforgiveness were eating away at "me," not anyone outside of this self-built wall. The bible states in Mark 11:25 (NLT), "But when you are praying, first forgive anyone you are holding a grudge against, so that your Father in heaven will forgive your sins, too." This was a scripture I had to meditate on. Being a new believer in Christ, I made prayer a part of my life. So after reading this scripture, I prayed God would help me in this area. Through a period of solitude and fasting, I had the strength to speak with Dave about my forgiveness to him for all that we experienced through our divorce. What a RELEASE!! There was such an overwhelming sense of peace I felt through this process.

During this period, I was on fire for Christ…I gave up the dance club scene, I was single, attending church, serving and sharing the love of Christ with family members, who had eventually surrendered their lives to Christ a couple of years later. There was a sense of freedom and peace like never before. As I look back on this time in our lives and I fast forward to 2005, God was preparing us for a re-encounter, restoration…little did we know.

In October of that year I was ready to commit to marriage again, and this was my prayer: "God, I'm ready to be married again to someone who loves me for me and who loves my son for who he is, but also, understands and respects that my son has a father who loves him." After this prayer, I believed for what I prayed and left it in God's timing. Then, in December 2005, I received a phone call, unexpected, from Dave. I wondered what was going on, and the first words that came out of his mouth were, and I quote, "Don't say a word, but just listen to what I have to share with you." As I listened, he shared his love for me and that God had been speaking to him about us remarrying. Jaw drop and silence were my reactions to what he shared through the entire phone conversation. I didn't say a word, until he was ready to end the call, and I simply said, "Good night." It was as if I had dreamed the entire phone experience. But the first thing I remembered was my prayer. Now, this required some serious quiet time with God, because I didn't know who, but I also never considered Dave to be the man God was sending into my life.

There was distance between us. I was in New Jersey and Dave in Florida, but that didn't stop what God ordained for His glory. We started to speak, probably every day, and Dave traveled to New Jersey frequently to visit. The time we shared with each other was incredible; there was peace and love I never experienced between us. But as time went on, in August of 2006, I was diagnosed with breast cancer. This was devastating to hear, but I refused to submit to it. Going through this was difficult, but I thank God for the overwhelming love and support from Dave, family and friends…I could not ask for a more supportive group of people.

We were still going strong, phone conversations, visits, and in the beginning of 2007 after speaking with my pastor, Rev. Ronald B. Christian, we started to attend marriage counseling at Christian Love Baptist Church. We made a commitment to ourselves to make this a priority, and we thank God we had pastors who worked with our schedules. We had a different perspective from our first marriage, and I give God all the glory for allowing us to be RESTORED to represent His Kingdom.

Maybe there's someone reading this who can relate to my story. I encourage you to let go of the bondage of unforgiveness. Forgive those who have hurt you; trust me, the forgiveness is not for them, but FOR YOU! This unforgiveness only eats away at you…that person most likely has moved on with their lives, leaving you in a state of bondage that can only be RELEASED when you RELEASE.

<u>Questions to Ponder</u>

1. Do you base your marriage on biblical beliefs? Or do you base your beliefs on the advice from the media on how marriage should be handled?

2. Do you give the best of yourself to your spouse?

3. How has conflict resulted in strengthening a weak point in your marriage?

4. Are you praying for your spouse? Are you praying with your spouse?

5. Do you allow yourself to freely forgive? Or do you hold onto unforgiveness against your spouse or anyone else? If unforgiveness is a challenging area in your life to deal with, have you prayed for God's help in this area?

Chapter 5

Dealing with Differences

"Many marriages would be better if the husband and the wife clearly understood that they are on the same side." Zig Ziglar

Dave

In August of 1988, we moved into our first apartment together, madly in love during our first marriage. Our landlord took our first month's rent to Atlantic City and gambled away our money, and we later found out our apartment was already in foreclosure. Soon our finances were under a major attack; the honeymoon was over and we were arguing about lack of funds. You will find out quickly that life has a way of thumping you on your head. Here, we have two individuals with two different mindsets, who need to co-exist in the same space. I had no idea about Matthew 7:26 (NLT), "But anyone who hears my teaching and doesn't obey it is foolish, like a person who builds a house on sand."

We started out with a shaky foundation, and let me tell you, the wind blew on our marriage, and the whole house came crumbling down over time. If you're going to have a successful marriage anointed by God, you must find a resolution to your marriage issues, not only to survive the storm, but to soar above the storm like an eagle. See, I was a handful; I gave my wife excuse after excuse for why I couldn't be the person she believed I was capable of being. I'd taken my wife for granted, not acknowledging much of what she did at home. I wanted my wife to be more understanding about my feelings, but I had to accept that we're just different; we simply failed to understand each other's love language.

We had a lot of fun together for most of our first marriage. There were also times when I felt like every time we had a disagreement, I needed to go fix things, and Roz was looking for me to understand her feelings and not react to everything, no matter how small it may be. I carried my feelings on my shoulders, so I would get angry and close down completely, until maybe a week later. Let me share a bit of advice to those looking to get married someday. When dating and kind of feeling each other out, during the courtship, show up 30 minutes late. You might be saying, "What, Dave, have you lost your mind?" No! You need to see how your mate reacts when they are 'Hot' with you. If they throw a glass of champagne in your face and call you every name in the book other than the name your parents gave you, you might want to reevaluate this relationship. I am not telling you to act like a jerk or be disrespectful. You need to have deep conversations with your girlfriend or boyfriend before you go further into this relationship.

Think of two trees being planted next to each other. I'm sure when driving to work, you may notice trees planted alongside the highway. Immature trees need planks, rope, and 2x4 pieces of wood to hold up each side of the tree. Trees must get the proper soil and enough water in their infant stages. The wind may blow, the storm will come, but the young trees can endure the process. Let me ask you something; who's holding you up? If you're going to live together and share each other's most intimate secrets, you need accountability in your life. Go find a couple who's married, whose marriage has been put to the test.

You need a couple in your life with a strong marriage to share with you some wisdom on how to love each other unconditionally, regardless of each other's opinion. Roots need time to mature, so they can go further down into the soil and wrap around each other. When the winter seasons of life approach, ask the right questions, and have the right attitude. Do you invest your soul into someone? If you're going to have a meaningful relationship with your spouse, you must get past the googly eyes, nice dress, nice smile, and be honest about how you feel about each other. I want you to say to each other, "It's okay to be different."

Take time out to study your mate and see areas of their life where they're opposite of you and talk about how you're able to be one unit. Always remember, we all are a work in progress, so keep the peace and know you are a major player in keeping your marriage strong. You both might be the blessing someone else may need to get through the turmoil that's going on in their lives.

Roz

Each person is an individual; as such, no two people can reasonably be expected to agree on everything. Being able to recognize this as a fact of life is one of the most important signs of maturity, and in this case, maturity in marriage. It is also the first step in learning how to resolve differences effectively and understand the negative and positive impact our differences can have on one another. We can allow the differences to bring us to a vulnerable posture to allow God to strip away all those things that do not bring Him glory.

But I didn't get this during our first marriage. One major hindrance to our first marriage was me trying to change Dave for my own egotistical desires, but what I eventually discovered was that, as a spouse, we are used by God for each other's development, to bring each other to the fullness of who God created us to be.

This was eye opening for me, because I had a strong will to do things my way, but I also had to realize my way was not always the right way. And what contributes to my strong will is having an aggressive personality, although I'm quiet; some term this as passive aggressive. But with that, I had to learn to compromise; simply put, I had to play nice. Thank God, as I look back over my life with Dave, I can truly say there has been a tremendous increase in my maturity, and it continues.

Funny, as I look back, it was crazy to think I could change my husband for my own desires. I used that experience as a learning lesson, because I knew I would get married again. What I didn't know was that it would be to the same guy...my lover and best friend. Whoever said God does not have a sense of humor or His mission will not be accomplished if you're obedient?

One of the major lessons I learned, because I became a student of my failed marriage, was the uniqueness of one spouse complements the other and brings a richness to the marriage. With that, God was preparing me for our divine re-encounter; little did I know it at the time.

If you're tempted to try to change your spouse to be more like you, I want to share with you an example that I share with couples, who are experiencing this self-defeating battle. Think about this for a second...two people with the same personality married to each other. This will probably be a very boring marriage or very dangerous. You know your mood swings and differences, so would you want to deal with you, your personality?

I want to encourage you not to 'try' to change the other for selfish desires; instead, learn ways to deal and compromise with your spouse. And most importantly, allow God to use you and your spouse to develop each other into your fullest potential to become all God has created you to be and do together for His Kingdom.

Oh, yes, **Kingdom Marriage**...You might have heard about the statistics on divorce being higher in the church than in the world. Whether or not this is true, we want to focus our efforts on encouraging the sanctity of a **Kingdom Marriage**. To elaborate on what I refer to as Kingdom Marriage, it's a marriage functioning, according to God's kingdom principles for marriage. The first principle to understand is marriage covenant, which I refer to in 'Chapter 2 - Let's Start from the Beginning.' It's a covenantal union designed by God for both partners to fulfill their divine purpose for advancing His kingdom. And to go deeper, I am going to share some additional principles/scriptures that we use as a foundation for marriage.

Some focus principles/scriptures (not an exhaustive list) on which we reflect to define a Kingdom Marriage:

1. **Marriage Covenant** – Mark 10:9 (NLT) "Let no one split apart what God has joined together."

2. **Patience & Forgiveness** – Ephesians 4:32 (NLT) "Instead, be kind to each other, tenderhearted, forgiving one another, just as God through Christ has forgiven you."

3. **Resist Temptation** – I Corinthians 10:13 (NLT) "The temptations in your life are no different from what others experience. And God is faithful. He will not allow the temptation to be more than you can stand. When you are tempted, he will show you a way so that you can endure."

4. **Trust in the Lord for your marriage** – Proverbs 3:5-6 (NLT) "Trust in the Lord with all your heart; do not depend on your own understanding. Seek his will in all you do, and he will show you which path to take."

5. **Sex Priority in Marriage** – I Corinthians 7:3-4 (NLT) "The husband should fulfill his wife's sexual needs, and the wife should fulfill her husband's needs. The wife gives authority over her body to her husband, and the husband gives authority over his body to his wife."

6. **Monogamy in Marriage** – Matthew 5:27-28 (NLT) "You have heard the commandment that says, 'You must not commit adultery.' But I say, anyone who even looks at a woman with lust already committed adultery with her in his heart."

7. **Love Each Other** – Ephesians 5:33 (NLT) "So again I say, each man must love his wife as he loves himself, and the wife must respect her husband."

8. **Marriage to Reflect Christ & the Church** – Ephesians 5:21-25 (NLT) "And further, submit to one another out of reverence for Christ. For wives, this means submit to your husbands as to the Lord. For a husband is the head of his wife as Christ is the head of the church. He is the Savior of his body, the church. As the church submits to Christ, so you wives should submit to your husbands in everything. For husbands, this means love your wives, just as Christ loved the church. He gave up his life for her."

As mentioned, these are only the tip of the iceberg of scriptures that reflect a Kingdom Marriage. As you review these scriptures and apply them to your marriage, you'll notice a sense of unity between you and your spouse…they reflect a marriage that looks less like the world and more like a Kingdom Marriage.

Knowing Who You Are:

As mentioned previously, I'm very passionate and a strong-minded woman. I share this again, because during our first marriage and during the first year of our current marriage, I had a very bad habit of shutting down completely when a situation was not in my favor in our marriage. This manipulation stemmed from childhood, and this controlling spirit had to be rectified. I used this as a retaliation and manipulation mechanism to control the situation. Yes, I would go to sleep angry, sleeping on the edge of the bed, and making sure we did not touch.

I created an atmosphere of mistrust.

I didn't allow Dave space to complain, and as a result, his dignity was lost in the disagreements. I believe spouses should be free to complain, not in a disrespectful way, but to share complaints as a healthy avenue to express their opinion and concerns, without the other shutting them down.

Side Note: Consistent complaining will not strengthen a marriage. There must be a healthy dialogue of praise of one another as well. This allows us to build each other's self-esteem. The bible says in Proverbs 18:21 (KJV), "Death and life are in the power of the tongue: and they that love it shall eat the fruit thereof."

A controller will make you pay a price for saying 'it' the way you (the spouse) felt. In this instance, I was the controller.

We dealt with this after it happened a couple of times during the first year of our current marriage. Dave sat me down to confront this issue. He let me know how detrimental this was to our marriage. It was this scripture that he confronted me with, one day, (Ephesians 4:26 NLT): "If you are angry, do not let it become sin. Get over your anger before the day is finished." There were many other times that he quoted this scripture, but this time it really caught my attention. I know this was the time the walls were down, and I was in a receptive posture to hear what my husband was saying. I'm not perfect, by any means, but **I'm committed to stay in a posture of being a student of my spouse**.

As my eyes were opened to this destructive behavior, I made an intentional decision to do a self-evaluation of my actions. This did not happen all at once, but I started where I was, and that was with an apology to my husband.

Nothing ever changes, unless I make a decision to change my response, and this came because of a renewed mind.

I started to pray about my actions and cry out to God to help me. I know I have a choice in how I react to situations. I can fan the flames of deterioration or use the fire to kindle the progression of our marriage. It was time out for blaming and pointing fingers; it was time for me to take ownership of how I handled my marital relationship.

I was not only a student of our relationship, but a student of who I am and how I react to different situations.

I learned when I got saved for real, in 2000, (yes, prior to that I thought everything was done in my own strength) prayer is a weapon to use to confront, to comfort, and to bring revelation right smack in the center of my situation. Now, I talk about prayer because my faith is what I base my beliefs on. So when faced with difficulties or ambiguity, prayer brings revelation to those situations.

Mind you, this was not always the case, but because of my faith and experiencing the power of prayer, this is a priority in my life. And I encourage every married couple, if you're not already, to incorporate this into your personal life and to share this precious time with each other.

I've discovered prayer is an equalizer that allows me to accept and deal with the differences between my husband and me. Even through the most challenging times in dealing with our differences, the Lord brings to my remembrance Philippians 4:6 (NLT), "Don't worry about anything; instead, pray about everything. Tell God what you need, and thank him for all he has done." During those times I pray for wisdom on how to deal with the differences. Sometimes, that wisdom is simply remembering that no two people can reasonably agree on everything, so I AGREE to DISAGREE but seek a middle point on which to compromise to find resolution.

Questions to Ponder

1. What are the greatest strengths of your spouse?

2. Do you accept and celebrate the differences of your spouse?

3. Do you think your spouse believes you're a team? If unsure, ask them.

4. Do you try to change your spouse? Or do you allow God to use you to cultivate and nurture the potential within your spouse?

5. Do you try to control your marriage with manipulation?

Chapter 6

Beware of Outside Voices

"Our background and circumstances may have influenced who we are, but we are responsible for who we become." Barbara Geraci

Dave

February is the chilliest time during the winter season in New Jersey. Roz and I would grab our winter coats, walk out into the cold Northeastern air, and I would remind myself, "I hate driving in snow and freezing rain. Why do I have to live in poverty, robbing Peter to pay Paul?" We were struggling to make ends meet. It seemed as though nothing was working the way we planned, and it felt overwhelming. I was speaking words of defeat.

You know, you have to be careful what you say out of your mouth. The bible says in Proverbs 18:21 (KJV), "Death and life are in the power of the tongue: and they that love it shall eat the fruit thereof." Beware of the words you say; don't sow a seed if you're not prepared to see a harvest. Most men will not admit that they're just scared little boys, who need their mommies. No outside forces can take you out, unless you believe the voices that are going on in your mind. If someone tells you, you're stupid, do you believe you're stupid? Don't believe those negative voices about yourself and don't believe those voices from others.

We currently live about 45 minutes away from Clearwater Beach, Florida. We enjoy the beauty of the palm trees, the flowers, and all that nature has to offer. One of the things we're looking to work on is having a nice garden. When we purchase the plants, they will have taken on the shape of the pots they're contained in, so if we want to see growth, we must take the plants out of their pots and place them into the soil. The taller the plants grow, the deeper the roots need to go. Do you want your marriage to grow, or do you want to limit the potential? You must treat your marriage with the love and affection that will prevent selfishness and pride from destroying your marriage. No outside forces can harm your marriage as long as your marriage is rooted and gets the right spiritual, emotional, and physical nourishment from God.

If you want God to bless your marriage, you need to have God in the center of your relationship, so you can become the light the world is hungry to see. You have to stay away from toxic people, who have evil conversations about your spouse, and are discerning when you get advice from family and friends. Make sure the opinions of others do not become your reality. Don't let someone else's problem become your problem. Monitor your conversations and be sensitive about fault finding from outside sources; make sure you take heed of this information, to build up your marriage and not tear it down.

Roz

I'm going to start with an experience we had that wasn't pleasant at all, but it's important to share some of the trials and tribulations we experienced. This happened, as we were in our separation stage, just before we divorced. There were tensions flaring, and I was not pleased with how things were going during our separation.

There was an incident where we had to stand before a judge, because I was very upset and didn't trust Dave at that time. Yes, there was adultery during our marriage. Yes, I was upset and did not appreciate the dishonesty, so I did a little private-eye stuff and found out he was seeing another woman. I confronted him on her property, and she called the police. Well, thank God, I didn't do anything stupid, but I did get a summons for trespassing. With that, we had to appear in court, and my mother was by my side. We were both questioned about the incident, and Dave came out and said I was being disruptive; my mother was so upset, and she let it be known. Oh, she was HOT over this! I had to calm her down. Like almost any parent, my mom was very protective of me and was really disappointed with us divorcing. So about 2 years (yes, it took this long) after we divorced, we came to an agreement that we would be moral and civilized in front of and for our son. And that's what we did. We tried our best to shelter our son from the emotional turmoil that we know so many children experience when parents divorce.

We eventually reached a level of camaraderie between us. Although it started out for the purpose of our son, we found that we could speak civilly to each other, and there was peace between us.

I share this story, because as a married couple, or in our experience, divorced, it's important, at some point, to forgive and move on, even if it involves family. I could have held a grudge, but I made a choice to move on, and eventually, Dave apologized to my mom, and she accepted his apology.

So, regardless of how long you and your spouse have been married, you may have noticed that over time, more and more people have begun to populate your lives. On the other hand, it is possible that you have not even noticed it or have not yet realized that it can have a significant impact on your marriage.

While it is a fact of life that your marriage cannot be "an island unto itself," the influence of other people can often prove to be quite challenging.

We're no different in respect to having a lot of people whom we know and love, but not everyone is qualified to know all our marital business. This was a trap we fell into during our first marriage. We freely shared confidential information about our marriage, instead of talking to each other. But, we also now know that was our immaturity, and we had to face any consequences of our actions. It's never the listener's fault, although we may confide in that person.

Only be transparent about something you're willing to yell from the top of a stadium.

Looking back, I thank God I learned from those experiences. Not everyone who has experienced divorce can say they have a second chance with the person they loved and can now use those bad choices as a learning barometer for a re-birthed opportunity. I don't take credit for what God has reunited, but I thank God I can reap the benefits.

One of the major reasons I believe we freely shared confidential information was that the other spouse 'was not there.' I take full responsibility for not making my husband a priority in my life. And I know there were times when I deliberately ignored Dave and his need for conversation.

Pushing him or driving him away only gave room for outside voices to penetrate our marriage. This, in turn, gave him ample opportunity to seek an ear from those who would listen. Needless to say, this was part of a bigger issue that led to our divorce.

I remember times when I would rather speak to friends or family members than speak with my husband. I'm not saying there's anything wrong with speaking to others, but when I made the mistake of putting more emphasis on having a dialogue with others, rather than with my spouse, then it became an issue.

Also, remember when I talked about me shutting down because of my controlling spirit? Yes, what I thought was controlling, in actuality, was a hindrance to our first marriage. We're talking about 'Beware of Outside Voices.' It may not have been a physical person, but I allowed a demonic voice to control my actions. The outside voices are, sometimes, those voices we allow into our thoughts to control how we act or react to situations. The bible says in Romans 12:2 (NLT), "Don't copy the behavior and customs of this world, but let God transform you into a new person by changing the way you think. Then you will learn to know God's will for you, which is good and pleasing and perfect." This is a scripture I have to remind myself of every time I experience a thought that contradicts God's word. Unfortunately, this wasn't the case during our first marriage, but I cling to this scripture now.

I encourage those who are married to know that the plan of the enemy is to steal, kill and destroy, but God's purpose is to give us a rich and satisfying life (paraphrased from John 10:10).

'Beware of the Outside Voices' that try to infiltrate what God has joined together, and my prayer is that your own voice does not come against your desire for the vision of your marriage. Remember, Proverbs 18:21 (KJV) states, "Death and life are in the power of the tongue: and they that love it shall eat the fruit thereof."

Create boundaries for your marriage!

Questions to Ponder

1. Do you speak words of defeat over your marriage? Or are you speaking words of hope?

2. Have you and your spouse discussed what you're willing to share with others outside of your home? (Note: this does not include abuse, physical or emotional; if you're dealing with emotional or physical abuse, you should confide in someone who's able to direct you in properly handling this situation.)

3. Do you confront or allow others to speak negatively about your spouse?

4. Do you freely give your spouse opportunity to have conversation with you, or do you push them away?

5. Do you monitor who speaks into or connects to your marriage?

Chapter 7

Hidden Treasures

"You must decide if you are going to rob the world or bless it with the rich, valuable, potent, untapped resources locked away within you." Myles Munroe

<u>Dave</u>

Thanksgiving Day is a time of giving thanks for the many blessings bestowed upon us and others, being appreciative for all we have. But instead of showing gratitude, we played the blame game, blaming one another for our dysfunctional lives. Most marriages spend a huge amount of time pointing the finger at each other; the real enemy you need to be aware of is the unseen forces. The evil forces tend to infiltrate one of your close friends, who smile in your face, but behind your back, they're laughing and rooting for us to walk away from our vows we made before God.

Let's look at the story about Adam and Eve in the Garden of Eden and try to learn some lessons from them. Adam and Eve disobeyed God by eating the fruit from the tree in the middle of the garden. God's command to them was, you can have any tree, except the tree in the middle of the garden. The bible says, in Genesis 3:9-13 (NLT), "Then the Lord God called to the man, where are you? He replied, I heard you walking in the garden, so I hid. I was afraid because I was naked. Who told you that you were naked? The Lord God asked. Have you eaten from the tree whose fruit I commanded you not to eat? The man replied, it was the woman you gave me who gave me the fruit, and I ate it. Then the Lord God asked the woman, what have you done? The serpent deceived me, she replied. That's why I ate it." Here, you have Adam finding fault with Eve, and Eve blames the serpent (devil). Neither one was willing to take responsibility for themselves; they would rather spend their energy faulting each other.

Oh, we were no different. During our first marriage, we would spend a massive amount of energy finding fault with one another. It was like a volleyball game. I would spike the ball then she would. In the end, nothing was resolved. I thank God for a renewed mind. Now we're committed to praying and understanding how to love and respect each other God's way. I made it my goal to love her the way God sees her, and let me tell you, a mighty miracle began to take place in her life. She was no longer the woman I married many years ago. She matured right before my eyes. She began to love me supernaturally. She stopped talking over me, and she began to listen to my needs. When you love God with all your heart, it should be evident in the way you treat your spouse. If you're dating and are looking to take things to the next level, your love for God will be evident in how you love people. If you are dating, I truly believe you should not lock lips until you make a vow before God to honor and love the person you're willing to spend the rest of your life with.

I know the world thinks you're crazy for thinking that way, but if you apply it to your life, you will discover treasure inside your mate. So many couples rush the process, because they bought into the lie that they need to get married before they get too old. You must take your time and get to know each other well enough to take it to the next level. I'm sure there will be some haters who will say you should have sex before you get married. Let me get real here for a quick minute: "No Ringy, No Dingy." Fellas, keep the car (body parts) in the garage and wait until the day of the parade (wedding day) for you to march your car down main street (altar). Ladies, keep that chastity pad on lock down and don't remove it until you have a man of God who's willing to ride and die with you. Don't allow any man who's not your husband to feel on your breast. Every part of your body is a hidden treasure, and the man or woman who is willing to go the extra mile and explore the forbidden caves must be willing to make the needed sacrifices before God.

You must not lower God's standards for anyone; don't let anyone make you feel guilty for waiting to get married before you become intimate, not just physically, but emotionally and spiritually, too. If you give up the goods before marriage and have sex, you will have to deal with the outcome. He or she may come up with some lame excuse why they're not ready to take it to the next level, because you gave up the goods. The longer we share our lives, the more God will begin to show the treasures that are on the inside of each person, but you must be obedient to God; He must be the center of your marriage and every other area of your life.

I want to leave you with this story as we wrap things up. Here is a story of a man who owned a field. He had rich soil, and the ground was very fertile. He went to town and heard a man say he found some diamonds on the other side of town. He thought to himself, let me go and plow my land, and maybe I will find some diamonds. He worked very hard, and he ran across some hard ugly rocks; he threw his shovel down in disgust and called the Realtor. He decided to sell his land, because he thought the land was not valuable enough. He sold his property and went to another town to invest in another field. The new landowner moved onto the property he had acquired from the ambitious landowner. He grabbed his shovel and started digging and found some hard ugly rocks, and as he looked closer, he noticed they were diamonds. These precious stones looked unattractive in their rough stage. God placed treasures inside your spouse; you need to dig deep and be unwilling to quit when you don't see anything. You must keep going, keep praying, keep giving of yourself to each other, and one day, when you least expect it, you will see the treasure manifest in every area of your lives. If you quit, like the ambitious landowner, you will never discover the hidden treasure.

Roz

'Hidden Treasures' are those things that are not readily seen or readily available, but can be found if we are intentional in seeking them. We must be willing to search, dig, and get dirty in the process. Although it takes a lot of work and patience, there are riches we would never find, unless we go through the process. We put our energy into what matters most, those treasures beneath all of the debris, rather than settling for the pebbles or those less attractive things found on the surface, most likely, what others have trampled over.

Remember, whatever you give attention to, you make important.

Oh, how often we find what we're looking for if we look hard enough. Many times, I sought all the faults I could find in my husband; guess what, I could probably give you a 2-page list or more. On the flip-side, who am I to point out all of his faults, when I have a ton of them, myself? But, as I'm maturing in my marital relationship, I choose to seek out the treasures that are hidden in my partner, my lover, my friend. I'm willing to go through the process; I give patience to what matters most to me.

I remember my focus went to the problem, instead of the promise. My perception was off. I was so focused on the problem, instead of seeing what God sees in my husband. Now, I see our marriage as a second opportunity of a lifetime. No, it isn't perfect, but I choose to seek the treasures in an imperfect man.

I didn't know the significance of my marriage. Now, being a student of my spouse, I 'choose' to see what I hadn't seen before. No, this does not happen out of the blue; it's intentional. Even as I step back to Chapter 5, 'Dealing with Differences', I wrote about how God uses our spouse to bring us to our fullest potential. That fullest potential is not only God stripping away what does not bring Him glory, but spouses discovering and cultivating those treasures within each other. I must see my spouse new every day. Heck no, it's not always easy, and it doesn't just simply happen, especially when we have disagreements. I would be deceiving you and myself to say that. But I will say; this is a process I have to continue to train myself to do.

As I'm writing this, I think of how much I enjoy the National Geographic Channel. You might wonder, Roz, what does that have to do with hidden treasure? Well, a lot. National Geographic Channel gives such a great analogy of the significance, patience, and passion archeologists have when excavating for rare artifacts. As they discover these rare finds, they share them with the world.

I use this analogy, because as a wife, I understand my role must consist of patience and passion to search and find the hidden treasures within my husband. When I started to cultivate and encourage those treasures that I discovered within him, not only did he become more attentive to my gifts, but we discovered more of how God began to use us as a unit.

I love this scripture, Lamentations 3:23 (NLT): "Great is his faithfulness; his mercies begin afresh each morning." As I meditate on this scripture and the mercies God gives me every morning, I also use this to cultivate my marriage. God gives me a blueprint for how I should provide the same mercies to my husband.

If God sees me new every morning, it's because of His love for me. So because of my love for my husband, I demonstrate grace and mercy. When I took on this mindset, not only did I change, but things changed. What a transformation from when we were first married. The harshness, the stubbornness, and the selfishness were far from grace or mercy.

Because I know He loves me, I use His example and instruction to love my husband. Although I thank God for the many successful marriages He has divinely connected us with, in man's humanity, he is still flawed. There's no greater example or guide to follow for a successful marriage than to follow the path Christ has set before us. His ways will help cultivate in us a relationship that will be an example for our future generations, a path of unconditional LOVE.

Although we know our experience is something we can share with future generations, we have realized God is using our trials and failures to encourage, equip, and support other marriages through their challenging times. It simply wasn't all about me anymore. Other hidden treasures started to surface from our mess, from the rubbish that was excavated from our first marriage. We believe God can use a mess and turn it into a miracle for all to see. And we're thankful for the opportunity allotted us to sow seeds of encouragement and support into other marriages.

Finding those 'Hidden Treasures' is a process, hard work, and sometimes, it gets pretty dirty, but through persistence, determination, unconditional love, and most importantly, God as the foundation, a marriage can be successful and a true witness for the Kingdom of God.

Questions to Ponder

1. Have you decided to love your spouse unconditionally?

2. Do you listen to the needs of your spouse?

3. **For the soon to be married folks** - Do you have premarital standards? Have you created boundaries to avoid having sex before marriage? Do you speak with your soon to be spouse about their dreams and aspirations?

4. Are you intentionally seeking ways to help your spouse fulfill their potential?

5. Are you allowing your spouse to cultivate and help you grow in your potential?

Final Words

Well, we hope we've accomplished our mission by sharing our story to encourage you to be relentless in your marriage. To fight for it, to stand firm, and most importantly, to allow God to be the center and foundation on which your marriage and life stand. We're not perfect, far from it, but we have experienced the good, the bad, and the power of having God in the center of what, sometimes, seems very difficult to bear. Also, know that God is in the restoration business... nothing is over, until He says so.

There are many challenges that we all may face as married couples, but a healthy and positive perception and perspective about the situation will allow us to persevere through the challenging times. We've discovered one of the most powerful things we can do to keep a right perspective concerning our marriage is to look in the mirror and ask ourselves the question, **"What is it like being married to me?"** We're not saying all situations will be easy, but we are saying that through prayer, support, a right perspective, and God in your life, you can stand against the darts of adversity.

About The Authors

Coach Dave captivates his audience from all walks of life, developing needed skills that will bring transformation to his listeners for generations to come through humor and visuals. He's well-received and loved by his students (mentees) and colleagues. As a Certified Personal Life Coach, author and speaker, Dave focuses on transforming the lives of people through goal setting, life planning skills, and accountability measures. He grew up in Northern New Jersey, surrounded by violence and poverty, with a loving sister and a mother, who instilled hard work and perseverance into their lives. After finishing high school, he joined the United States Army and later met his wife, Roseline 'Roz' during his college years; they are blessed with one son, Terrell. Dave took a wrong turn in life and discovered problems, heartache, and disappointment do not discriminate. He lost everything that was dear to him and made a decision to seek God for healing and restoration.

Now, he empowers countless individuals in his surrounding community and shares his faith and love for

God with many individuals from diverse cultures. He has also committed himself to empower, encourage, and bring hope to our youth who have made mistakes and who've found themselves detained within local juvenile detention centers. In 2012, he was ordained as an Evangelist, and he travels around the world encouraging people to live on ***PURPOSE***.

Roz has teamed up with her husband, Dave, to encourage and empower marriages. They've found, through their own challenges, first being married for 8 years to each other, then 10 years of divorce, and now as they write this book, 8 years remarried, when each spouse puts the other first...**No One is Left Out**. After being asked to plan married couples' fun and engaging events, which they felt unqualified to do, they eventually realized that through these activities, marriages became more passionate, and everyone had lots of fun. Their passion is to encourage and empower marriages through fun and engaging workshops.

Along with her passion for seeing marriages strengthened and having fun, Roz has mentored numerous young adults through the Development School for Youth. She mentors married women, and she's an author, publisher, and fitness enthusiast, who's passionate about inspiring and helping women create and sustain a Fit Lifestyle. She has found, because women are natural nurturers, they put everyone else before themselves, causing them to put their fitness on the back-burner.

Now she and her husband, Coach Dave, have teamed up to structure fun and engaging marriage workshops and bootcamps that will connect couples on another level. The workshops and bootcamps are designed for interaction...they've moved away from the typical marriage conferences, where couples gather, sit, and listen. These bootcamps and workshops are for married couples to INTERACT and have FUN! Their **marriage bootcamps and workshops** are based on Biblical principles.

COACH DAVE BENNERMAN
CEO & Founder of Ignite Your Vision Now

Other Exciting Titles
by Ernest Dave Bennerman
"Get Fired UP! About Your Life Because If You Don't, Who Will?"

Visit Coach Dave & Roz's Website at:
www.igniteyourvisionnow.com

www.ingramcontent.com/pod-product-compliance
Lightning Source LLC
LaVergne TN
LVHW051150080426
835508LV00021B/2570